DERBY COUNTY – FOOTBALL LEGENDS

Michael Cockayne

© Michael Cockayne
First published in the United Kingdom, 2006
Stenlake Publishing Limited
54 - 58 Mill Square
Catrine
KA5 6RD
www.stenlake.co.uk

ISBN 9781840333640

A contribution from the sale of each book is being donated to the Kidneys For Life charity:
for more information visit www.kidneysforlife.org

The publishers regret that they can not supply
copies of any of the pictures featured in this book.

Foreword.

I first watched Derby County in October 1966 when they defeated Millwall 5-1 at the Baseball Ground. Tim Ward was the manager at the time, and although the crowd of around 17,000 went home happy, nobody realised just how much the football club would change in the years that followed.

Brian Clough arrived and twice within the space of four seasons, I joined the thousands who witnessed the Rams parade firstly the Second Division title, and then the "Big One " - the First Division Championship - around the town centre.

This book is not, however, meant to be just a celebration of the good times. It is more intended to be a brief introductory history to the triumphs, tragedies and heroes of one of the oldest clubs in the country.

Although the Rams current position is depressing, as a fan I can still dream ... of again seeing an open-top bus carrying a Derby County team enjoying yet another major success.

MICHAEL COCKAYNE, 2006.

Acknowledgements

A number of people have kindly provided images for this work. Thanks are due firstly to Ian Hayes of the Ramstrust, and Neil Hallsworth for allowing me to use items from their own private collections. Thanks also to Carol Seal at the Derby Evening Telegraph, Stuart Marshall of Collectors World, Glasgow, Nick Tomlinson from the Picture the Past website - www.picturethepast.org.uk - Mr Burrows at the Derby Local Studies library, Sporting Heroes www.sporting-heroes.net and last but not least Nigel Mercer.

Derby County were formed in the summer of 1884, the football club coming into existence as an offshoot of Derbyshire County Cricket Club. Home matches were contested at the County Ground on Nottingham Road, and the team's colours initially matched those of its cricketing counterparts - amber, chocolate and light blue. The Rams first game was on 13th September 1884, but in an inauspicious start they were beaten 6-0 by Great Lever. Over the 1886 - 1888 seasons Derby played a variety of challenge matches, as well as competing in the County Cup and the Football Association Cup. The early luminaries of the club included George Bakewell and Benjamin Ward Spilsbury, the latter having also played for the famous Corinthians side. The overall standard of the Rams challenge matches tended to improve after their 2-0 defeat of Aston Villa in November 1885, the game attracted an estimated 5,000 to the County Ground with the goals coming from Smith and Evans.

The Rams record goal scorer Steve Bloomer. As well as accumulating over 330 goals for the club, he also scored 28 times in 23 appearances for England.

As the game became more organised, the Rams were elected as one of the twelve founder members of the Football League which was established in Manchester on April 17th 1888. For the record, the eleven other clubs were : Accrington, Aston Villa, Blackburn Rovers, Bolton Wanderers, Burnley, Everton, Notts County, Preston North End, Stoke, West Bromwich Albion and Wolverhampton Wanderers.

An early picture of the Rams team - note the Victorian penchant for a moustache.

FOOTBALL LEAGUE 1888/89

	GP	W	D	L	GF	GA	PTS
PRESTON	22	18	4	0	74	15	40
ASTON VILLA	22	12	5	5	61	43	29
WOLVERHAMPTON	22	12	4	6	50	37	28
BLACKBURN	22	10	6	6	66	45	26
BOLTON	22	10	2	10	63	59	22
WEST BROM	22	10	2	10	40	46	22
ACCRINGTON	22	6	8	8	48	48	20
EVERTON	22	9	2	11	35	46	20
BURNLEY	22	7	3	12	42	62	17
DERBY COUNTY	22	7	2	13	41	61	16
NOTTS COUNTY	22	5	2	15	40	73	12
STOKE	22	4	4	14	26	51	12

After enduring a difficult first Football League season, the Rams, who finished 10th and needed to seek re-election, made two significant signings which helped shape their destiny for the next decade. The well publicised arrival of the Goodhall brothers - John, from the 'Invincibles' at Preston and Archie from Aston Villa boosted attendances at the County Ground to an average of just under 4,000. The cup tie with Everton on January 18th 1890 was, however, witnessed by an estimated 10,000 people, with the Merseysiders coasting to a very one sided 11-2 victory. The collapse of the Derby Midland club enabled the Rams to further strengthen their resources, but when a pale-faced teenager made his debut in September 1892, few realised that football had found its first real superstar.

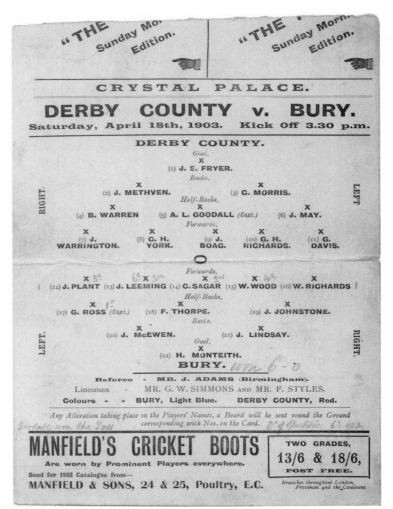

The 1902/03 Cup Final programme. Although the Rams were beaten 6-0 by Bury, they were hampered by goalkeeper Jack Fryer taking his place in the side despite being clearly unfit. Fryer eventually left the field after 68 minutes when the Lancashire club were 4-0 ahead.

More action from the Rams 1904 Cup game with Blackburn. The players take their positions ahead of a Derby corner kick.

Steve Bloomer, born in Cradley Heath but educated in Derby, scored eleven goals in the 1892/93 campaign. Although John Goodhall tallied three more, Bloomer emerged as the Rams top marksman in all but one of the next thirteen seasons. His ability enabled Derby to become one of the strongest sides in the country, their 3-1 FA Cup Final defeat by Nottingham Forest in April 1898 marking the first of a trio of Cup Final appearances in six years. Unfortunately, all three games ended in defeat, and with the Rams also being beaten in four semi-finals between 1896 and 1904, many believed that the Baseball Ground, their home from September 1895, had been cursed by local gypsies. Francis Ley a local industrialist owned the land, giving it the distinctive name after being captivated by the American sport on a visit to the United States. He spent a considerable sum improving the facilities, to the extent that by the turn of the century the Rams were able to attract crowds of 20,000 to their biggest games.

Team picture 1908-9 season

Back row:	J. long, W.J. Nicholas, H. Maskrey, C. Morris
Middle row:	J. Methven (Manager), E. Scattergood, T. Barbour, B. Hall, A. Latham (Trainer), G. Richards, J. Bagshaw
Front row:	G.A. Thompson, E. Trueman, F.W. Bevan, A. Bentley, H. Barnes, J.W. Davis, J.W. Edwards

Despite the increase in attendances, finance remained a problem and, to avoid an impending crisis, Bloomer was sold to Middlesbrough in March 1906 for £1,000. With the Goodhalls having also departed, after 661 appearances and 137 goals between them, the transfer brought to an end the Rams first successful era. Although the trio had gained the majority of the plaudits, several others, in particular Jack Robinson, Jimmy Methven, Jack Cox and Johnny McMillan, also made huge contributions to the club's fortunes during the 1890s. In the summer of 1906 Methven was appointed as the Rams first manager free of administrative duties, but without their talisman and record goal scorer, Derby proved to be no real match for many of their opponents once the 1906/07 campaign got underway. They were relegated after winning only nine of the 38 league matches, and after nineteen years faced life outside of the top flight for the first time. Although Methven's side then managed to stay amongst the leading Second Division clubs for several seasons, it was only Bloomer's return in September 1910 which heralded a revival.

STEVE BLOOMER - DERBY COUNTY RECORD 1893 - 1914

YEAR	GAMES	GOALS
1892/3	28	11
1893/4	27	19
1894/5	31	11
1895/6	30	27
1896/7	33	31
1897/8	26	20
1898/9	33	30
1899/1900	30	19
1900/01	28	24
1901/02	36	18
1902/03	26	13
1903/04	35	25
1904/05	30	13
1905/06	26	12
1910/11	32	24
1911/12	38	19
1912/13	30	14
1913/14	6	2
TOTAL	**525**	**332**

A plaque erected to celebrate Steve Bloomer's achievements.

In 1911/12 he captained the team to promotion whilst forming an excellent strike partnership with Jimmy Bauchop, the duo netting 34 league goals between them. In a topsy-turvy spell, Derby survived two seasons before again being relegated, only then to regain their status in 1914/15; the campaign which proved to be the last before league football was suspended because of the First World War.

After the hostilities, the Rams initially relied on a mixture of youth and experience but, with Bloomer long retired and finances tight, goal scoring became a problem. After narrowly avoiding the drop in 1919/20, the 1920/21 campaign proved to be a disaster. Only five games were won, and with Bill Paterson, a £3,000 mid-season arrival from Cowdenbeath, topping the scoring charts with eight, relegation was an inevitability before the final day 3-0 defeat at Manchester United. Worse still, Methven was suffering from failing eyesight, and after the 12th place finish in 1921/22 he left the club. It was a sad end for the man who had arrived at the club as a player from St Bernard's in 1891.

Team picture from 1914
Back row: L-R ATKIN, BARBOUR, SCATTERGOOD, BUCKLEY, WALKER, WAUGH
Front row: L-R GRIMES, MOORE, FORDHAM, BARNES, FELLOWS.

Cecil Potter was installed as the new manager, the former Hartlepool United boss bringing defenders Tom Crilly and Harry Thoms with him to the Baseball Ground. Potter only spent three seasons in charge, but was twice close to winning promotion back to the First Division. Despite a tight budget, he recruited well, and in his first campaign the Rams also battled through to the semi final of the Cup, a crowd of over 50,000 witnessing their 5-2 defeat by West Ham United at Stamford Bridge.

Below: A share certificate issued in 1923. The Rams had planned to move to a new home at the Municipal Sports Ground, but instead opted to purchase the Baseball Ground for £10,000 from Sir Francis Ley.

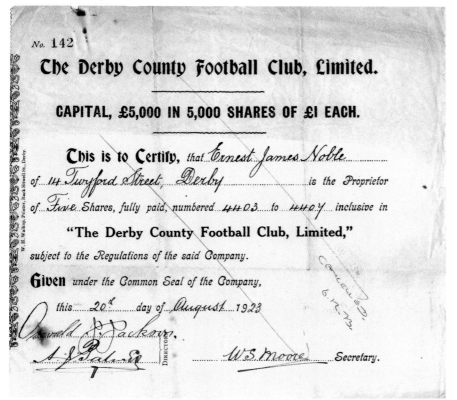

Above: Caricature of Harry Thoms who played 195 games for the Rams before joining Crystal Palace with Crilly and Jimmy Gill.

Potter's decision to leave heralded another new era for the club. Under the management of George Jobey, a tough no-nonsense Geordie, the Rams returned to the First Division after the 1925/26 campaign. The signing of Harry Bedford from Blackpool for £3,250 proved crucial, his 27 league strikes enabling Jobey's side to accumulate 77 goals - equalling the club record which had been set in 1908 thanks to an identical haul by Alf Bentley.

Left: Harry Bedford was signed by George Jobey in September 1925. Over six years with the club Bedford scored 152 goals in 218 appearances, a total which included a quartet in three games and a further 10 hat tricks.

Right: Johnny McIntyre the £10 signing from Stenhousemuir in 1921: a bargain for a man who was a key member of the line–up for a decade. Regrettably his career was beset by injury, without which he would surely have played more games.

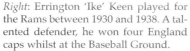

Left: Bobby Barclay was recruited by George Jobey from non league football and scored three goals when the Rams defeated Sheffield Wednesday 4-1 in April 1930.

Right: Errington 'Ike' Keen played for the Rams between 1930 and 1938. A talented defender, he won four England caps whilst at the Baseball Ground.

By the end of the decade Jobey had transformed the Rams, and they again emerged as one of the strongest sides in the country. Although success in terms of silverware eluded them, their reputation for playing exciting attacking football meant that an array of international players were persuaded to wear the Derby shirt. Jobey was always looking to improve his squad, to the extent that the modern game would have dubbed him a 'wheeler dealer' - an average season witnessing a dozen or more transactions in the transfer market. The 2nd place finish in 1929/30 saw Bedford hit the 30 goal mark, and with Sammy Crooks, Bobby Barclay and George Stephenson also recording double figured tallies, fans at the Baseball Ground saw their favourites beaten only once.

A rare picture from the Rams end of season tour to Germany in 1934. The players were instructed to give a "Nazi" salute to their hosts, something they reluctantly agreed to - with the notable exception of goalkeeeper Jack Kirby.

As well as bringing established performers to the club, Jobey also used his contact network superbly. Jack Barker and Jack Bowers, for example, were signed for a few hundred pounds apiece after opposing each other in a Midland League fixture. Bowers, a brave whole hearted centre forward, eventually replaced Bedford as the focal point of the Rams attack. He set a new scoring record in 1930/31 with 37 league goals, a total which included quartets against Chelsea (6-1), Portsmouth (5-1) and Manchester United (6-1).

When Bowers was badly injured early in the 1935 campaign, Jobey brought the legendary Scottish forward Hughie Gallacher to the Baseball Ground. It proved to be a shrewd short-term signing. Gallacher, despite being past his best, still netted 40 goals in 55 appearances, including all five against Blackburn Rovers in December 1934. The Rams again finished runners up in 1935/36 and 6th in 1938/39, the final full season before war was declared.

Left: Jack Bowers emerged as one of the most consistent scorers in the Rams history - his 220 appearances yielding a magnificent tally of 183 goals. After ending his career with Leicester City, he returned to Baseball Ground as part of the back room team.

Right: When Bowers was sidelined by injury, Hughie Gallacher proved to be a more than capable replacement. Sadly Gallacher met a tragic end. After a series of problems, he committed suicide by throwing himself in front of an express train in 1957.

The programme cover for the game at Chelsea in October 1938. The Rams won the contest 2-0 with their goals coming from Dai Astley and Ronnie Dix - both men having arrived at the Baseball Ground from Aston Villa. In later life Astley coached, most notably, Sampdoria and Internazionale Milan.

Many people wondered how Jobey managed to attract so many top players to the Baseball Ground. In 1941 part of the reason was revealed. The Rams were found guilty of accounting irregularities going back to 1925 and fined £500. Several directors were also suspended, with Jobey being banned from management. Football resumed in Derby on Christmas Day, although in Jobey's absence it was largely left to Jack Nicholas to organise the playing activities. Games throughout the wartime period were however dependent on the appearance of guests from a variety of clubs, with results often determined by who was available on the day.

Left: Douglas 'Dally' Duncan came to the Baseball Ground in 1932. Over the years that followed, he proved to be a fine goal–scoring winger, netting 69 goals in 289 appearances.

Right: Although Jack Nicholas was born in Derby, he represented Wales as a schoolboy. However, when it came to his adult career there was only one club for Nicholas or 'Owd Nick' as he was known on the Popular Side. In Derby's first 122 years he was the only skipper to lift the FA Cup.

In 1944 Ted Magner was appointed as the Rams new manager, and the following year, thanks to the regular presence of performers of the calibre of Raich Carter and Peter Doherty, both established internationals, Derby won the Football League North title and the Midland Cup.

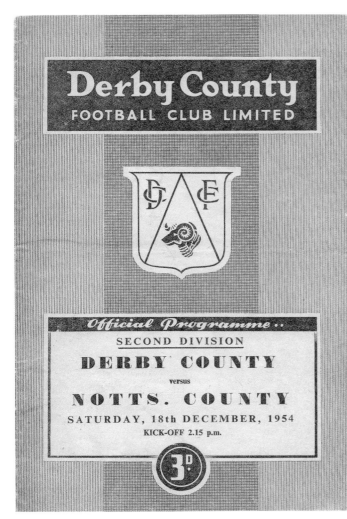

Left: Programme for game against Notts County in 1954. Tommy Powell scored the Rams goal in a 1-1 draw. Powell, who emerged during the war years, was followed into the Baseball Ground by his son Steve - between them the pair made a remarkable 826 appearances for the club.

Right: Reg Harrison was the 'baby' of the 1946 team, but went on to serve the Rams superbly over the years that followed. He was the top scorer in the 1948 campaign, and in a 281 game career netted a total of 59 goals.

In peacetime, each round of the 1945/46 FA Cup was, up to the semi final stage, contested on a home and away basis. With Carter and Doherty now officially Derby County players: Carter having been transferred from Middlesbrough and Doherty from Manchester City, the Rams surged through the early stages with aggregate defeats of Luton Town (9–0), West Bromwich Albion (4–1) and Brighton and Hove Albion (10–1).

Left: A ticket for the 1946 Cup Final, a competition which captured the public imagination after the war years.

Right: The cover of the programme.

With Magner having surprisingly left for an overseas coaching job, it was left to Stuart McMillan, the son of the famous Rams striker from the 1890s, to lead the club to Wembley. After overcoming Aston Villa and Birmingham City his side, which included locally developed Tommy Powell, Leon Leuty, Chic Musson and Reg Harrison defeated Charlton Athletic 4-1 (after extra time) in the Final. Jackie Stamps, another big brave centre forward, netted a brace and also burst the ball ... as 98,125 witnessed the first final since 1939. Nicholas received the trophy from King George VI, a tremendous reward for a player who made 383 appearances for the club.

Jack Parr (Left) broke his arm just before the Wembley final, and was replaced at left back by Jack Howe (Right). Between them the two Jacks made over 370 appearances for the club. During the war, Howe served with the Cameron Highlanders, and guested for Hearts, Falkirk, Aberdeen and St Mirren. He was also one of the first sportsmen to wear contact lenses.

As fans flocked back to the game in the late 1940s, the Rams twice broke the transfer record. Scot Billy Steel was recruited from Greenock Morton for £15,000, and later another forward, Johnny Morris, arrived from Manchester United for £24,500. The duo were viewed as the longer term replacements for Carter and Doherty, but Steel, a complex character, appeared to unsettle the dressing room, and by the end of 1952/53 both record arrivees had departed. As a consequence, Derby were relegated after collecting just 32 points, their lowest total since the 1921 campaign.

Second Division football saw the return of Jack Barker as manager. Unfortunately, he inherited a team that relied too heavily on its ageing performers. The Rams slipped down to 18th in 1953/54, and then bottom twelve months later. Despite spending a significant amount in the transfer market in a last ditch attempt to avoid the drop, Barker's side still finished five points adrift of the rest and once a second relegation in three seasons was confirmed, he was told that his undistinguished spell in charge was over. He was replaced by Harry Storer, a stalwart of the 1920s Baseball Ground line up. Ahead of the Rams first ever campaign outside of the top two divisions, Storer returned to his former employers at Coventry to sign Reg Ryan - a tough tackling inside forward who was immediately installed as club captain. Although Derby enjoyed a largely successful 1955/56 campaign, they missed out on promotion after finishing 2nd behind Grimsby Town. Jack Parry was the leading marksman with 24 goals, but controversially he missed the last 11 games after being badly injured during the 3-1 defeat by Grimsby on March 10th 1956.

An early 1950s style Rams home programme.

The tough tackling Frank Upton spent two spells with the Rams and in all made 272 appearances.

The way things used to be...Upton's contract for the 1959/60 campaign.

Within the year Storer's side went one better and regained their Second Division status. They were crowned champions after a season which saw Ray Straw net 37 goals to equal the club record set by Jack Bowers in 1933/34. Straw's haul enabled the Rams to record in excess of 100 league goals for the second successive year, their total being boosted by a 7-1 Easter Monday mauling of Chesterfield. Unfortunately Storer had limited funds at his disposal to strengthen the squad even further. Over the five seasons that followed the Rams were never better than a mid table team, and at the conclusion of the 1961/62 campaign Storer announced his retirement at the age of 64.

Under the management of Tim Ward between June 1962 and May 1967, the Rams again struggled to make an impact on the Second Division, the 8th place finish in 1965/66 representing their highest placing. In his defence Ward, who had earned two full England caps during a 260 game career at the Baseball Ground, was, like his predecessor restricted by the Board's reluctance to release cash. Significantly, he did however persuade the Welsh duo of Alan Durban and Eddie Thomas to join the club. Those two signings, respectively from Cardiff City and Swansea Town, came ahead of Ward's major legacy to the Rams - his long desired capture of Kevin Hector from Bradford in September 1966.

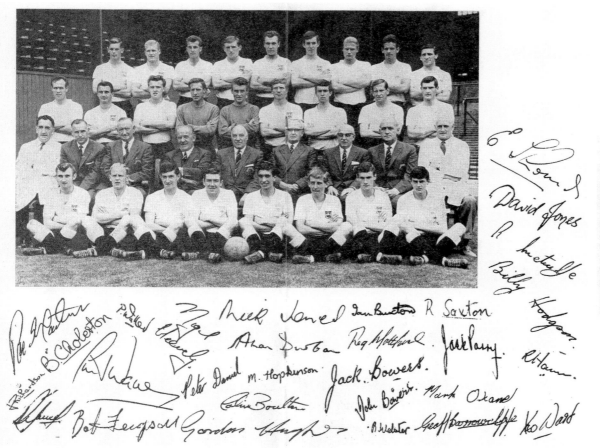

DERBY COUNTY
SEASON 1965-66

Back row (from left): P. Daniel, R Ferguson, R. Young, P. Waller, T. Rhodes, K. Ward, M. Hopkinson, R. Webster, W. Hodgson. *Second row*: G. Barrowcliffe J. Parry, R. Saxton, R. Matthews, C. Boulton, A. Durban, N. Cleevely, E. Thomas, J. Bowers. *Seated*: Ralph Hann (trainer), Mr. T. Ward (manager), Mr. S. Longstone, Sir Robertson King (president), Mr. H. Payne (chairman), Mr. B. J. Walters, Mr. S. C. Bradley, Mr. R. Kirkland, Jack Bowers (assistant trainer). *Front*: J. Richardson, G. Hughes, R. Metcalfe, M. O'Kane, W. Cholerton, P. Boyer, M. Jones and J. Nixon.

Autographed 1965/66 team picture.

Left: Reg Mathews joined the Rams from Chelsea in October 1961. A brave acrobatic goalkeeper - seen here challenging Billy Bremner of Leeds United in the 1968 FA Cup 3rd Round.

Right: The front cover of the programme for the 1st leg of the 1968 League Cup semi final. Leeds eventually defeated the Rams 4-2 on aggregate, with the contest at the Baseball Ground attracting over 31,000 - a game decided by a penalty, needlessly conceded, by Bobby Saxton.

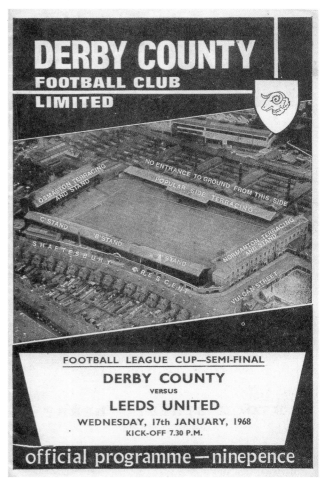

Already a proven goal scorer in the Fourth Division, Hector cost the best part of £40,000. It was a huge fee for a club of Derby County's size to pay, but one which was recouped many times over as 'The King' (as he was quickly christened by the fans) went on to make a record breaking 581 appearances. His pace and balance also enabled him to net 201 goals, easily enough to place him behind only Bloomer in the all–time scoring charts.

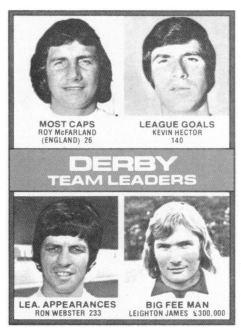

A collectors card from the mid1970s

Despite sixteen strikes from Hector in 1966/67, several bouts of rash defending meant Derby slumped to 17th place, and Ward became the latest to be informed that his contract would not be renewed. He was replaced by Brian Clough, a brash young manager, who immediately stated his intention to transform the entire club. With his assistant Peter Taylor, Clough soon spent £75,000 to sign John O' Hare, Roy McFarland and Alan Hinton, a trio of players who would become great servants to the Rams. It was not, however, until the arrival of Dave Mackay and Willie Carlin twelve months later that Clough's promise came to fruition.

Alan Hinton played on the left wing between the 1968 and 1976 campaigns. A superb crosser of the ball, his ferocious shooting also added 83 goals from 316 appearances.

The Rams 1968/69 team picture.
Back row L- R Burkitt (trainer), Wignall, Walker, Durban, Green, Robson, McFarland, Webster.
Front row L -R McGovern, O'Hare, Mackay, Hector, Carlin, Hinton.

With the inspirational Mackay captaining the side from his role as sweeper, Derby won the Second Division title at a canter by five points. A crowd of 31,644 flocked to the Baseball Ground on April 29th 1969 to see the team celebrate their success with a 5-0, last day of the season, demolition of Bristol City. Home League Cup victories over Chelsea and Everton, both leading First Division clubs, suggested that Clough's new look line up would hold its own in the top flight. Their 3-1 replay win against Chelsea has long been a part of Rams folklore, goals from Mackay, Durban and Hector in the final thirteen minutes capping a magnificent team display.

Left: Willie Carlin (8) celebrates with Hector after scoring against Millwall.

Above: Mackay proudly displays the 1968/69 Second Division trophy.

The Rams enjoyed a superb 1969/70 campaign. Their 4th place came after a series of particularly impressive results at home, the First Division newcomers accounting for Mackay's former club Tottenham Hotspur (5-0), Liverpool (4-0) and Manchester United (2-0) amongst a total of fifteen Baseball Ground victories. Unfortunately, another enquiry into the Rams administration prevented Clough going on to test his side in the UEFA Cup. After being found guilty of irregularities, Derby were fined £10,000, and banned from all European games for a year. It was a harsh price to pay, but Clough was not a manager to be denied for too long.

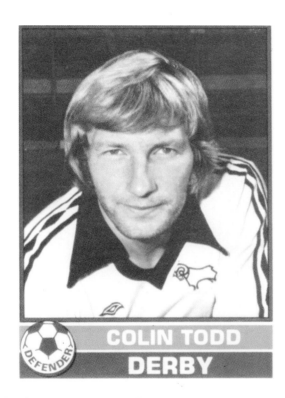

COLIN TODD
DEFENDER
DERBY

The Watney Cup
FINAL
DERBY COUNTY v. MANCHESTER UTD.
Saturday, 8th August, 1970
OFFICIAL PROGRAMME ONE SHILLING

Although 9th place twelve months later was a disappointment, the First Division championship was secured in 1971/72. With Colin Todd, signed for £175,000 from Sunderland, replacing Mackay in defence, and Archie Gemmill now anchoring the midfield, the Rams stayed with the pace setters throughout. They completed their schedule with a 1-0 home victory against Liverpool, and were relaxing in the sunshine of Calla Millor when news broke that their nearest challengers, the Merseysiders and Leeds United had both failed to win their final fixtures.

After being denied the chance to play against European opposition, the Rams turned their attentions to the Watney Cup. They defeated Manchester United 4-1 in the final, and then shared eight goals with the Old Trafford club in the league fixture on Boxing Day. The Christmas game marked a last Rams appearance for goalkeeper Les Green who was dropped after United came from behind to earn a point.

Kevin Hector (*Left*) and Ron Webster (*Right*) vital members of the two Championship winning teams. Both men went on to make well over 500 appearances for the Rams, with Hector additionally scoring 201 goals. His haul included five in a UEFA Cup–tie against Finn Harps and a further six hat tricks.

The Rams were unable to defend the title in 1972/73, with their league placing of 7th being a consequence of an extended run in the European Cup. Ahead of the competition, Clough strengthened his defensive options by signing David Nish from Leicester City. The fee of £225,000 set a new British transfer record, and was a throwback to the late 1940s when the Rams twice broke the record within the space of twenty months. The midweek European ties certainly produced a marvellous atmosphere at the Baseball Ground, aggregate victories against Zeljenicar, Benfica and Spartak Trnava setting up a mouth-watering semi-final clash with the Italian giants Juventus.

Right: The programme cover for the game in Czechoslovakia against Slovan Bratislava in the 1975/76 European Cup.

Medzinárodné futbalové stretnutie

O POHÁR MAJSTROV EURÓPSKYCH KRAJÍN

SLOVAN CHZJD BRATISLAVA

DERBY COUNTY

Štadión Slovana na Tehelnom poli

17. septembra 1975 ·   19.30 hod.

Above: A ticket for the European Cup semi final game against Juventus in Turin.

After losing the first leg in Turin 3-1, Derby faced an uphill task in the return tie on April 25th 1973. Additionally, they had to play the 'Old Lady' without McFarland and Gemmill, both of whom were suspended after innocuous bookings on Italian soil. As it transpired, Juventus opted to stop the Rams at any cost, a missed penalty and the dismissal of Roger Davies ensuring that the final whistle sounded with the scoreline still blank.

ROY McFARLAND - DERBY COUNTY
RECORD 1968 - 1984

YEAR	GAMES	GOALS
1967/68	41	2
1968/69	51	9
1969/70	48	6
1970/71	41	2
1971/72	47	4
1972/73	53	7
1973/74	44	4
1974/75	4	0
1975/76	48	3
1976/77	45	4
1977/78	26	1
1978/79	27	3
1979/80	22	0
1980/81	24	3
1981/82	-	
1982/83	-	
1983/84	4 (5)	0
TOTAL	**522 (5)**	**48**

Signed from Tranmere Rovers by Brian Clough for just £24,000, McFarland proved to be one of the finest defenders in the Rams history. Had injury not disrupted his career, he would have earned many more than his 28 full England caps.

Having seen Clough and Taylor achieve so much, supporters were devastated to hear that the duo had resigned in October 1973. A simmering dispute between Clough and the Board, particularly with Sam Longson and Jack Kirkland, erupted in the wake of a 1-0 defeat of Manchester United. Within a matter of days the Baseball Ground became a hub of media attention. What followed was unprecedented. The players threatened to go on strike, a fans' protest movement held demonstrations ... and Clough issued a writ against the club for libellous comments.

Left: Bruce Rioch scored fifteen league goals in 1975, a remarkable tally for a midfield player.

Right: Rod Thomas was signed by Dave Mackay, with the Welsh international defender going on to make 118 appearances for the club.

After the furore settled, Dave Mackay rejoined the Rams as manager. His strength of character shone through as, after failing to win any of the opening eight games that he was in charge, Derby recovered their poise and finished the year in an impressive 3rd place. Mackay had stated from the the outset that he would not panic buy new players. He kept his word, and within nine months his shrewd negotiating skills had secured the services of Bruce Rioch, Rod Thomas and Francis Lee.

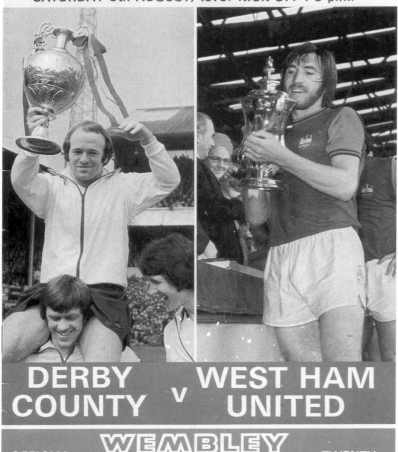

After being crowned champions, the Rams met West Ham United in the Charity Shield contest at Wembley - goals from McFarland and Hector earning them a 2-0 victory. The front cover of the programme shows Archie Gemmill (on the shoulders of David Nish) with the Championship trophy.

His plans for the 1974/75 campaign were, however, thrown into disarray when McFarland damaged an achilles tendon whilst playing for England. It left the centre-half on the sidelines for all bar the last four fixtures. In his absence, Peter Daniel stepped up to partner Todd at the heart of the defence and, somewhat unexpectedly, the Rams again emerged as Championship contenders. A maximum six point Easter, which included Davies scoring all five goals against Luton Town, left Mackay's side in a strong position – their title again being confirmed without the players kicking a ball. Ipswich Town failed to defeat Manchester City in their last game, the news coming through as the Rams squad enjoyed the annual end of season awards ceremony in the town centre.

Left: Derby were defeated 2-0 in the 1976 FA Cup semi final at Hillsborough, a game which effectively ended the era of them being one of the strongest teams in the country.

Right: Charlie George was signed ahead of the 1976 campaign. He is seen here challenging Alan Hansen of Liverpool at Anfield.

With the prospect of a European Cup campaign ahead, Mackay signed Charlie George for £100,000 before the start of the 1976 season. It proved to be a marvellous piece of transfer activity. Although the Rams exited the European competition 6-5 on aggregate to Real Madrid - that after a George hat trick had given them a sensational 4-1 home advantage - they produced a series of excellent displays in the league and FA Cup. Indeed, had the former Arsenal striker not dislocated his shoulder against Stoke City on March 24th 1976, Derby might well have clinched 'the double.' As it transpired they had to be content with another 4th spot in the Championship, their dreams of reaching the Cup Final being ended at the semi final stage by Manchester United.

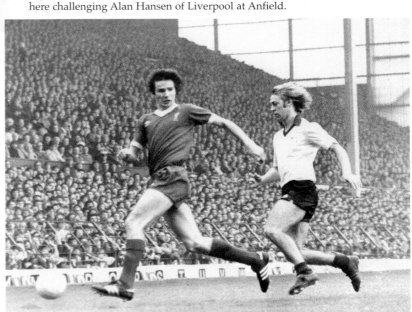

Below: Goalkeeper Colin Boulton won Championship medals under both managers, and appeared 344 times for the club. He was also the only player to appear in all 84 league matches over the two title campaigns.

Above: Brian Clough, who along with Dave Mackay is the only manager to have won the championship with the Rams.

When Mackay found himself criticised after a poor start to the 1976/77 campaign, he asked the board for a vote of confidence ... and resigned, along with his assistant Des Anderson, when it was not forthcoming. Bizarrely, it meant that the Rams had lost the two managers who had won them the Championship, both within eighteen months of the success being achieved.

Tommy Docherty was appointed manager in place of Colin Murphy. Unfortunately, his signings did little to halt the Rams decline and he departed at the end of the 1979 campaign. Most famously, he described the midfield trio of Gerry Daly, Don Masson and Bruce Rioch as his 'three Van Gogh's'...

To compound the departures, the choice of Mackay's replacement shocked the footballing world. Rather than pursue a big established name, the directors opted instead to promote Colin Murphy from the reserve team. Murphy made a significant signing in Gerry Daly, but his £300,000 acquisition of Derek Hales from Charlton proved to be an albatross around his neck - the bearded centre-forward scoring just seven goals in thirty games. The Rams finished 15th in 1976/77, thanks largely to a Daly inspired run of form which resulted in just two defeats in the last seventeen matches.The former Manchester United player also netted seven goals including a brace against Everton.

The Rams issued a special edition match day magazine to celebrate their centenary year. The cover for the game against Charlton Athletic on January 2nd 1984 featured the 1946 Cup Final team and Kevin Hector sporting an international cap.

When Murphy lost his job after a dismal start to the 1978 campaign, his successor Tommy Docherty offloaded Hales for little more than £100,000, a huge loss for a club lurching towards the wrong end of the table and an impending financial crisis. Docherty's activity in the transfer market was at times impossible to fathom. He rapidly sold the majority of Mackay's team and replaced them with inferior performers, to the extent that when he left in May 1979 the Rams were in 19th place. The damage took a long time to rectify. The inevitable drop to the Second Division followed with Colin Addison in charge and then, despite employing a succession of managers John Newman, Peter Taylor and Roy McFarland, the decline continued. More poor signings and a desperate lack of cash, which in April 1984 left the club within hours of being wound up, meant that by the conclusion of the 1983/84 campaign, the Rams again faced life in oblivion - 21st place resulting in relegation to the Third Division.

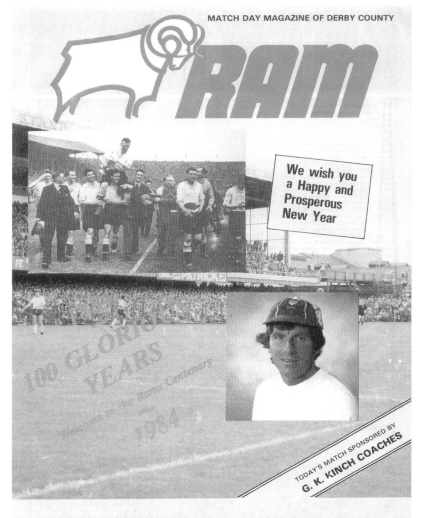

MATCH DAY MAGAZINE OF DERBY COUNTY

RAM

We wish you a Happy and Prosperous New Year

100 GLORIOUS YEARS

Welcome to the Rams Centenary

1984

TODAY'S MATCH SPONSORED BY G. K. KINCH COACHES

v **CHARLTON ATHLETIC,** CANON LEAGUE (DIVISION TWO)
MONDAY, JANUARY 2, 1984   3.00 p.m.   NUMBER THIRTEEN   50p

Bobby Davison netted 106 goals for the Rams in 249 appearances.

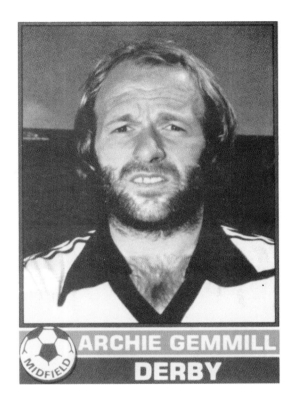

Arthur Cox emerged as the next new manager, his first move being to appoint McFarland as his right-hand man. Although Derby finished 7th in their first season under Cox's management, they won promotion twelve months later with Bobby Davison netting a total of 23 goals; the second season on the trot that the South Shields born forward had exceeded the twenty goal mark.

Left: Ted McMinn was a long term target of Arthur Cox. Signed from Seville for £300,000, the Scottish midfielder became hugely popular with the Rams fans.

Right: Rob Hindmarsh holds aloft the 1987 Second Division trophy. Hindmarsh was a commanding centre half who captained the side during two promotion campaigns.

With Cox then able to utilise part of the money that was injected via the Maxwell media empire, 1986/87 proved to be a memorable year. The Rams surged back to the top flight as champions after gaining 25 victories, including impressive home defeats of Grimsby (4-0),Brighton (4-1) and Plymouth (4-2). The contest against Argyle confirmed the title and attracted 20,798 to the Baseball Ground - a turnout that witnessed Nigel Callaghan, Gary Micklewhite and John Gregory, all shrewd Cox acquisitions, score in the last ten minutes.

The Rams promotion to the Premiership saw the arrival of Peter Shilton (*Above*) and Mark Wright (*Right*). The duo added the experience the squad needed, and proved vital in the battle to survive.

Ahead of the 1988 campaign Robert Maxwell took over as Chairman and promised big signings. Davison, the most saleable asset, moved on to Leeds United for £350,000 but Peter Shilton and Mark Wright, both senior England internationals, arrived from Southampton. However, without a real goal scorer, the Rams scraped to 15th place, after at one stage having lost eight matches in a row. Even at the age of 38, Shilton earned more than his fair share of points and celebrated a record 825 league appearances in the penultimate game at Watford.

Paul Goddard enjoyed a successful sixteen months with the Rams after being signed for £425,000. Seen here against Queens Park Rangers, Goddard netted 18 goals in 63 appearances.

Derby County enjoyed their best season for 13 years in 1989. Their 5th place relied heavily on the goals and enthusiasm of Dean Saunders, a £1 million transfer from another Maxwell club Oxford United, who quickly established a solid partnership with the former West Ham and Newcastle frontman Paul Goddard. However over the following two years, Cox found his options limited as the money supply dwindled and then eventually dried up. The Rams ended 1990 in 16th place and were relegated in 1991. The low point of the latter campaign was undoubtably an embarrassing 7-1 home defeat by Liverpool, with Saunders, somewhat predictably, netting his side's only goal.

Given their financial plight, the Rams were forced to sell their best players ahead of the 1992 campaign. Saunders and Wright went to Liverpool for a combined fee of around £5.1 million, which was just about enough to satisfy the Maxwell family. Cox again used the funds available to him well and bolstered his defence with the acquisition of Andy Comyn and Simon Coleman. In the end, 3rd place was better than might have been expected, but a huge injection of capital from local businessman Lionel Pickering certainly helped, particularly so once Marco Gabbiadini and Tommy Johnson were in the side.

The entrance to the Baseball Ground, the Rams home for 102 years.

Programme cover for the 1993 Anglo–Italian Cup Final when the Rams were unfortunately defeated by Cremonese. Derby also took part in the competition in both 1993/94 and 1994/95, with Kitson in all scoring nine goals in 11 appearances. He proved to be a marvellous acquisition, but finance eventually dictated his departure to Newcastle United for £2.25 million.

Sadly, the relationship between Pickering and Cox started to sour during the 1993 campaign. After spending over £5 million in as many months, the final position of 8th in Division One (1992/93 heralded the start of Premiership football) was a huge disappointment. An FA Cup run to the 6th round proved to be an unexpected fillip, as did the appearance in the Anglo-Italian Cup Final at Wembley. Paul Kitson led the overall scoring with 24 goals, including a marvellous autumn run of ten in thirteen league outings.

Another visit to Wembley....but again disappointment. Despite opening the scoring with a goal from Tommy Johnson, the Rams were beaten 2-1 - with the Leicester winner coming in the 87th minute. Johnson made 121 full appearances for the club and netted 41 goals. He left the Rams to join Aston Villa with Gary Charles.

A severe back problem forced Cox to step down early in 1993/94, with McFarland taking over the reins. His side managed to improve on that 8th place and the Rams did at least make the promotional play–offs. Pickering was, however, expecting a place in the Premiership as the reward for his investment. The subsequent 9th place in 1995 resulted in McFarland losing his job within half an hour of the penultimate match. It was a humiliating way to treat the man who had devoted the majority of his adult life to the football club.

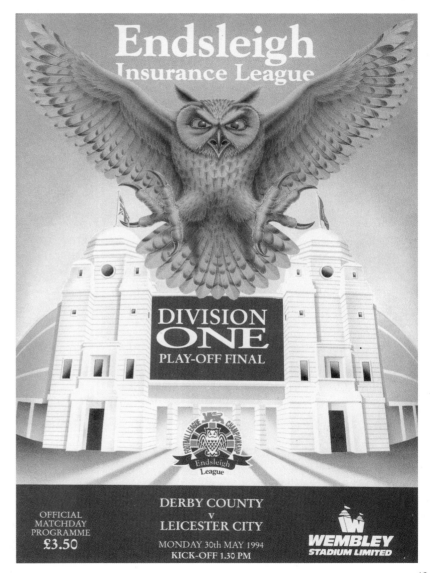

After interviewing several candidates, the Board appointed Jim Smith as their new manager ahead of the 1996 campaign. With a number of players determined to ply their trade away from the Baseball Ground, the first objective was to reassemble a competitive squad, a task Smith performed admirably well. His most influential signing was that of Igor Stimac who cost £1.57 million from Hajduk Split. The Croatian defender made his debut in a 5-1 defeat at Tranmere, but then inspired the club to a twenty game unbeaten run. Smith's side were eventually promoted as runners up behind Sunderland, with Dean Sturridge netting an impressive tally of twenty league goals.

Igor Stimac proved to be one of the Rams best signings of the 1990s. Stimac proved his international calibre at the highest level. As one of five Rams players to appear at the 1998 World Cup, he guided his beloved Croatia to a magnificent third place.

Arsenal provided the opposition for the last game at the Baseball Ground, with the front cover of the programme recalling the past with images of Steve Bloomer, Raich Carter, Jackie Stamps, Brian Clough, Kevin Hector and Dave Mackay.

The Rams held their own in the Premiership and ended the 1996/97 campaign in 12th place. The last game of the season against Arsenal also marked the end of the Baseball Ground era - the Gunners' 3-1 victory being unable to dent the air of nostalgia and sentimentality which surrounded the occasion. Over the following two seasons, with Smith utilising the expanding overseas market well, Derby continued to progress, their 8th place in 1999 being far better than the experts had predicted. Deon Burton emerged as the top overall score, with 12 - a tally that was the lowest total since the 1987/88 campaign. On the international stage Burton did however defeat cricketer Courtney Walsh and sprinter Merlene Otty to win the 1996 Jamacian Sports Personality of the Year.

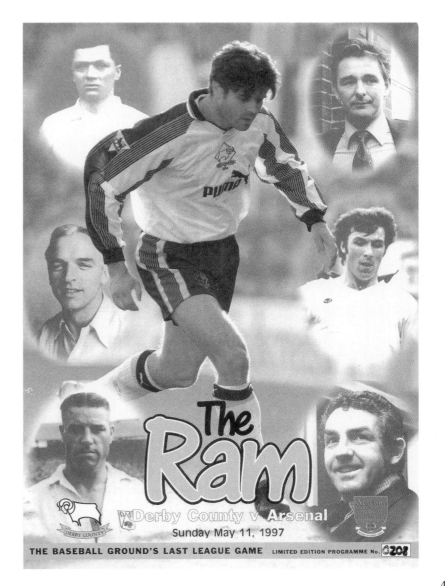

The Ram
Derby County v Arsenal
Sunday May 11, 1997
THE BASEBALL GROUND'S LAST LEAGUE GAME   LIMITED EDITION PROGRAMME No. 0208

It proved however to be the highspot. Finance was playing an ever important role in the game, to the extent that given the attendances at their new Pride Park home, the Rams found it almost impossible to compete with the bigger clubs. Goal scoring also became a problem; Rory Delap led the way in 2000 with eight, and despite Smith still being able to produce periodic master signings like Taribo West, a poor start to the 2002 campaign cost him his job. His replacement, another Baseball Ground favourite, Colin Todd lasted for just fifteen Premiership matches before himself being ousted in favour of John Gregory. The change made little difference as the club again lurched into crisis. Relegation followed and when the Rams, by then under the charge of George Burley, finished 18th in Division One in 2003, the stars of the Premiership side had been all disposed of ... in the name of balancing the books.

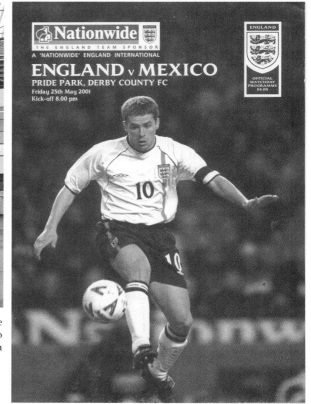

The entrance to Pride Park, a plush new facility which was considered to be of a standard to stage international matches - as indicated by the programme cover for the May 2001 England v Mexico fixture. Note the half mast flags and floral tributes at Pride Park after the announcement of the death of Brian Clough.

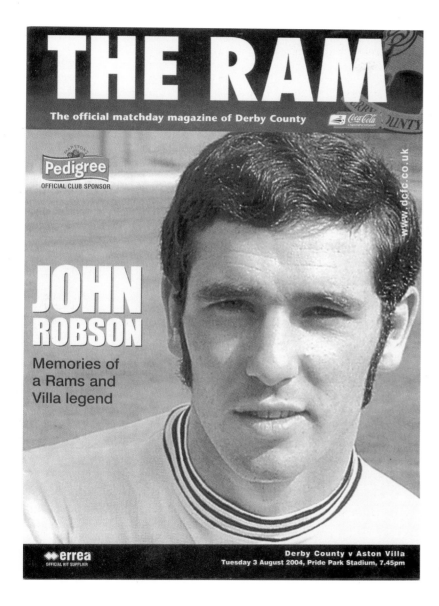

A poignant moment - the programme for the game against Aston Villa in August 2004 celebrated the career of John Robson, who had played for both clubs before losing a long battle against multiple sclerosis. Robson was signed from junior football in the north east and went on to represent the Rams in 211 matches between the 1968 and 1973 campaigns. He became surplus to requirements when Clough signed David Nish. When Robson subsequently moved to Villa, the fee of £90,000 was at the time a new incoming record for the Rams.

With new owners in charge, but still no money to spend, Burley steadied the ship in 2004 before overseeing a remarkable revival twelve months later. With a side totally dependent on loan and free signings, he guided the club into 4th place and the play-offs. Two players stood out: Polish forward Grezrgorz Rasiak scored sixteen league goals, whilst midfielder Inigo Idiakis controlled the midfield and provided a constant supply of accurate free kicks and corners. However, rather than getting praise for his achievement, Burley instead found himself subjected to stories about his personal life... it surprised nobody when he opted to walk away from the situation.

Another sad occasion as fans pay their respects to Clough. His popularity was such that over 15,000 people subsequently attended a memorial service at Pride Park. Gerald Mortimer summed up Clough's contribution to football when he said "We shall not see his like again."

As the book went to press, Billy Davies had been named as the Rams manager, with his appointment coming after a new consortioum headed by Peter Gadsby took control of the club.